IT's Raining Fish!: COOL FACTS ABOUT THE WEATHER

by Kaitlyn Duling

Raintree is an imprint of Capstone Global Library Limited, a company incorporated in England and Wales having its registered office at 264 Banbury Road, Oxford, OX2 7DY – Registered company number: 6695582

www.raintree.co.uk
myorders@raintree.co.uk

Text © Capstone Global Library Limited 2020
The moral rights of the proprietor have been asserted.

Edited by Meg Gaertner
Designed by Becky Daum
Production by Colleen McLaren
Printed and bound in India

ISBN 978 1 4747 7460 4 (hardback)
ISBN 978 1 4747 8245 6 (paperback)

British Library Cataloguing in Publication Data
A full catalogue record for this book is available from the British Library.

Acknowledgements
We would like to thank the following for permission to reproduce photographs: iStockphoto: diatrezor, 22–23, hadynyah, 12–13, Ji Feliciano, 7, 28, petesphotography, 26–27, Placebo365, 21, Wavebreakmedia, 30–31; Shutterstock Images: Caleb Holder, 14–15, fibPhoto, 8–9, Jeff Gammons StormVisuals, 5, John D. Sirlin, 18–19, MDay Photography, 17, PrabhatK, 25, Romolo Tavani, cover (bottom), Tony Campbell, cover (top), Yurio1978, 11
Every effort has been made to contact copyright holders of material reproduced in this book. Any omissions will be rectified in subsequent printings if notice is given to the publisher.

We would like to thank Dr Elinor Martin, Assistant Professor of Meteorology, for her help with this book.

CONTENTS

CHAPTER ONE
WILD WEATHER 4

CHAPTER TWO
BURNING UP AND COOLING OFF 6

CHAPTER THREE
CLOUDS AND WIND 10

CHAPTER FOUR
STORMS ON THE HORIZON.................... 16

CHAPTER FIVE
FALLING FROM THE SKY 20

Glossary 28
Trivia.................................. 29
Activity 30
Find out more 32
Index.................................. 32

WILD
Weather

Some storms are made of dust. Lightning burns hotter than the Sun. Clouds can drop frogs along with water. **Weather** is always changing. It is powerful. It is wild. Extreme weather can be amazing!

One hundred lightning bolts hit the Earth every second.

BURNING UP AND
Cooling Off

The Earth's hottest day happened in California, USA. It was 10 July 1913. The place was **Furnace** Creek. The temperature reached 56.7 degrees Celsius (134 degrees Fahrenheit)!

DEATH VALLEY

Furnace Creek is in Death Valley, USA. This is in the Mojave Desert. Death Valley is one of the Earth's hottest places.

Despite its heat, Death Valley is a national park and visitors go there every year.

7

The city of Verkhoyansk, Siberia, experiences the greatest temperature range in the world.

ICY DESERT

Antarctica may be cold. But it is still a desert. It does not get much rain or snow.

BRRRR!

Earth's coldest place is in Antarctica. Record lows happen in a mountain range there. The lowest temperature was taken by **satellite**. It was -93 degrees Celsius (-136 degrees Fahrenheit). People do not live there. But people do live in very cold places. Towns in Siberia get harsh winters. Temperatures can drop to -68 degrees Celsius (-90 degrees Fahrenheit).

CHAPTER 3

CLOUDS
and Wind

Clouds can come in crazy shapes. Some clouds look like layers of discs. They sometimes look like **UFOs**. Other clouds look like they have been hole-punched. A brief snowstorm can affect part of the cloud. It leaves behind a hole in the cloud.

Lenticular clouds
can look like UFOs.

MOUNT EVEREST

Mount Everest is the world's tallest mountain. Jet streams hit its peak. People who climb to the top feel the jet stream.

WIND POWER

The strongest winds happen miles above the Earth's surface. **Jet streams** are very fast winds. They can move at 440 kilometres (275 miles) per hour. Aeroplane pilots try not to fly against these winds. They fly above the jet stream. Or they fly in the same direction as the wind.

Climbers of Mount Everest face very cold winds.

Dust storms occur
mostly in dry areas.

Wind can whip up sand, dirt or dust. It can turn into a storm. These storms are called "black **blizzards**". They can happen all around the world.

DUST STORMS

Dust storms happen on other planets too. Scientists have seen dust storms on Mars.

CHAPTER 4

STORMS on the Horizon

A **hurricane** is a type of **tropical** storm. Its winds can flatten houses. Hurricane Irma struck in 2017. Its winds covered an area larger than England. They moved at 298 kilometres (185 miles) per hour.

Hurricanes can produce **tornadoes**. Hurricane Ivan hit the United States in 2004. It created 127 tornadoes. Tornado outbreaks can be dangerous. One happened in 2011. Over three days, 349 tornadoes struck 21 US states.

Hurricanes can cause massive amounts of flooding.

ZAP!

Lightning bolts strike during storms. They are bright and hot. In fact, they are five times hotter than the Sun! They can reach 27,700 degrees Celsius (50,000 degrees Fahrenheit).

Lightning starts in the clouds. Most of it stays there. But some bolts strike the ground. They zap at 300,000,000 kilometres (200,000,000 miles) per hour!

Thunder is the sound made by lightning.

CHAPTER 5

FALLING FROM the Sky

Rain and snow often fall from the sky. But strange things have also "rained" down onto the Earth. They include frogs, fish, snakes and meat. The cause can be a waterspout. This is similar to a tornado. But it forms over water. It lifts things in its path. Then it drops them like rain elsewhere.

WATER WATCH

Waterspouts are spinning columns of water. The water does not come from the sea. It comes from the clouds.

Many waterspouts form in the Florida Keys, USA.

Most hail falls as tiny balls of ice.

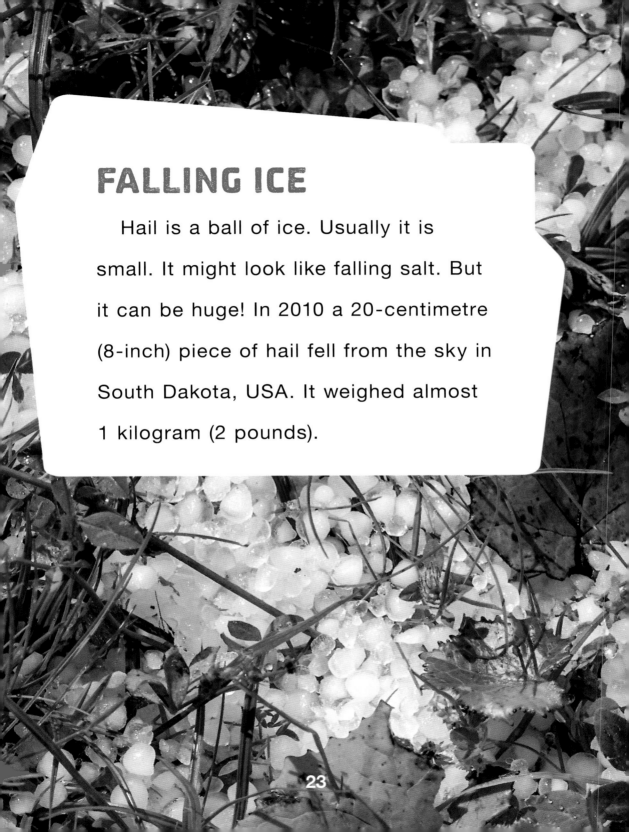

FALLING ICE

Hail is a ball of ice. Usually it is small. It might look like falling salt. But it can be huge! In 2010 a 20-centimetre (8-inch) piece of hail fell from the sky in South Dakota, USA. It weighed almost 1 kilogram (2 pounds).

SNOW MOTION

Some people make snowballs in the winter. But sometimes snowballs make themselves. Wind blows across a snowy field. It pushes the snow along a path. The snow forms a ball and rolls. It leaves a trail behind itself. These giant snowballs are called snow rollers.

Snow rollers are also known as snow doughnuts.

Snow can roll itself. Fish can fall from the sky. Hurricanes can be larger than countries. Weather is all around us. It can be amazing!

Supercell thunderstorms can bring large hail, strong winds and tornadoes.

GLOSSARY

blizzard
a harsh snowstorm with strong winds

furnace
a structure used to heat things to high temperatures

hurricane
a large tropical storm that includes circular winds

jet stream
a fast-moving river of air high in the sky

satellite
a man-made object that moves around the Earth

tornado
a strong column of wind that spins quickly

tropical
having to do with the tropics, the region of the Earth near the equator

weather
conditions that include heat, cold, storms, clouds, pressure, wind, moisture and more

UFO
an unidentified flying object, sometimes claimed to be an alien spaceship

TRIVIA

1. During hot summers in the northern hemisphere, it might feel like the Earth is close to the Sun. But it is the opposite. Earth is closest to the Sun during winter. Earth is furthest from the Sun during summer. The distance to the Sun does not create Earth's seasons. Earth's tilt on its axis does. The tilt affects the angle at which the Sun's light hits Earth.

2. Some thunderstorms actually produce snow instead of rain. This is called "thundersnow".

3. Chinook winds blow east from the Rocky Mountains in the US. They bring warm air during winter months. They are sometimes called "snow eaters". They get rid of snow quickly. They are named after the Chinook Native Americans.

ACTIVITY

WEATHER TRACKER

Scientists study the weather. They take careful notes and measurements. You can study the weather too. Choose a city in another country. You can compare the weather at home and in that city.

Study the weather for one week. Pay close attention to the weather in your neighbourhood. Take the temperature every morning, at noon, and at night. Write down if it rained or snowed. Were there clouds, or was the sky clear? Look up the pressure and humidity too. Write down your findings in a chart. You can include drawings or photos.

At the same time, study the weather in the other city. Look up the weather information online. Make a chart for that place too. When the week is over, look at your two charts. How was the weather in the two cities the same? How was it different?

FIND OUT MORE

Interested in wacky weather? Check out these resources.

Books

50 Things You Should Know About: Wild Weather, Anna Claybourne (QED, 2016)

Totally Amazing Facts About Weather, Jaclyn Jaycox (Raintree, 2018)

Websites

DK Find Out!: Weather
www.dkfindout.com/uk/earth/weather

Met Office: Weather for kids
www.metoffice.gov.uk/learning/weather-for-kids

INDEX

Antarctica 8, 9

clouds 4, 10, 18, 21

dust storms 15

Furnace Creek 6, 7

hail 23
hurricanes 16, 26

jet streams 12, 13

lightning 4, 18

Mount Everest 12

rain 8, 20

snow 8, 10, 20, 24–26

temperature 6, 9
tornadoes 17, 20

waterspouts 20, 21

INTRODUCTION

Edinburgh Corporation and its direct successors, Lothian Region Transport from 1975 and Lothian Buses from 2000, liked to operate a largely standardised double-deck fleet. Between 1952 and 1966 it had bought 446 Leyland Titans, followed by 588 Atlanteans between 1966 and 1981, so it was probably inevitable that the Olympian would become the standard double-decker for the Lothian bus fleet in the 1980s and 1990s when it bought 430 examples from Leyland and Volvo.

Lothian had been tempted by Leyland to order two integral TN15 Titans, but the order was cancelled as a result of the continuing uncertainties over the model, and two of the new Olympian model were supplied instead. They were very early examples – chassis ON42 and ON43 – and were in many ways updated versions of the last Atlanteans delivered just five months earlier. The Atlanteans were 9.5m long with Leyland 680 engines; the Olympians were 9.6m long with the TL11 engine, the turbocharged version of the 680. The Atlanteans and prototype Olympians had two-door Alexander bodies with 75 seats, though the seats were differently distributed.

Nos.666/667 were to be the only 9.6m Olympians bought new by Lothian. Buoyant passenger numbers had tempted Lothian to look at bigger buses. A long Preston Atlantean had been tried in service in April 1981 and Lothian was convinced that this was the way to go. So the first proper batch of Olympians, delivered in 1983, were 10.3m long examples. The extra length was just one factor that marked them out from the rest of the fleet; the most important difference was that they had Eastern Coach Works (ECW) bodies, built at Lowestoft.

Walter Alexander, based in Falkirk, Edinburgh's and Lothian's main body supplier since 1961, had been less than amused when Leyland's successful one-stop shopping bid included its in-house ECW bodywork. Questions were

asked at very high leve business outside Scotla Alexander continued to business and was rewarded with the bodywork order for the 1988 batch of 36, and would go on to build the bodywork on all of Lothian's Olympians – 300 of them – for the next decade or so.

The move to Alexander bodywork coincided with a change of engine supplier. With the future of Leyland's engines in doubt, Lothian turned to the Cummins L10 engine coupled to a ZF gearbox, which proved to be a successful combination in the fleet.

The 1994 delivery of Olympians looked broadly similar to previous batches, but were built at Irvine by Volvo, and badged as Volvos. The 1996 Olympians were very different. They not only had Volvo engines, they also had Alexander Royale bodies, which introduced a more rounded and contemporary look to Lothian's fleet. The 1997 batch were to be Lothian's last Olympians; they brought Lothian's Olympian fleet to 430 vehicles, though there were never that number in the fleet at one time, as the first no.770 only stayed briefly with Lothian before being bought back by Leyland as a demonstrator, and no.666, the diabolically-numbered first Olympian for Lothian – was burned out in 1987.

The Lothian Olympians were good buses, bridging the generation between the last of the Leyland Atlanteans and the first of the lowfloor Dennis Tridents. The last of the breed, the 67 Alexander Royale-bodied Volvo Olympians represented the ultimate incarnation of the step-entrance rear-engined double-deckers bought by Edinburgh Corporation and Lothian since 1965. If the move to lowfloor buses had not come along in the late 1990s, Lothian would doubtless have continued to buy constantly improving versions of the Olympian/Royale.

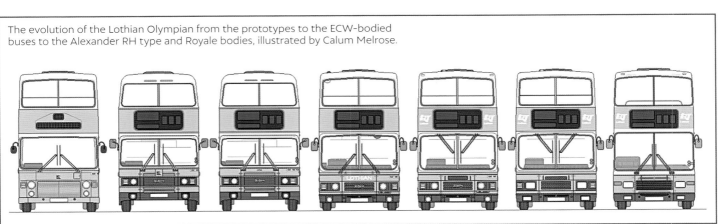

The evolution of the Lothian Olympian from the prototypes to the ECW-bodied buses to the Alexander RH type and Royale bodies, illustrated by Calum Melrose.

THE TWO PROTOTYPES

666/667   GSC-X   ONTL11/1R   ALEXANDER H47/28D

The first two Lothian Olympians arrived in April 1982 – probably supplied by Leyland at a good price following the cancelled Titan order and to get the new model's foot in the door of Leyland's best municipal customer. Nos.666/667, following from the last Atlanteans rather than taking up the vacant numbers allocated to the two Titans (599/600), had 75-seat two-door Alexander RH bodies, and were roughly to the same layout as the last two-door Atlanteans.

They had Bristol-built chassis with Leyland TL11 engines, the turbocharged successor to the 680 engines in all of the Atlanteans delivered to Edinburgh Corporation and Lothian between 1972 and 1981.

Both had what were then fairly novel electronic destination displays – 666 provided by Transign and 667 by Luminator. These provided a restricted display when compared with the standard LRT layout, and in 1984 both received larger and clearer Vultron electronic displays. No.666 was withdrawn following a fire in 1987 but 667 stayed in service until 2000, latterly with conventional front destination blinds; it is now preserved.

Although 666 was withdrawn after a fire in 1987, 667 survived in service until 2000, with a more legible (if on this occasion poorly set) standard Lothian destination display and wheelnut guard rings. It is now preserved. It was photographed at Pilton layover point in June 1999.

The second of Lothian's two prototype Olympians, 667, had a different style of destination display, by Luminator, rather meagre compared to Lothian's normal offering. It is seen in Princes Street in June 1982, with a recently-delivered Eastern Scottish Olympian/ECW following.

Numerically Lothian's first Olympian, Alexander RH-bodied 666 in its original form, with an early Transign LED destination layout and lacking wheelnut guard rings on the front axle. No.666, newly into service in April 1982, is seen in Leith Street.

No.666 as originally delivered, in Lothian Road in April 1982.

THE FIRST ECWs

668-702   OFS-Y   ONTL11/2R   ECW H50/31D

Five months after LRT's first Olympians, delivery started of a batch of 35 more Olympians, but these were very different to 666/667. Leyland, with Eastern Coach Works (ECW) and Charles H Roe as in-house bodybuilders, was keen to sell complete vehicles to operators, and if these couldn't be Titans, then operators might be attracted by competitive prices and guaranteed deliveries as a result of one-stop shopping. All 35 were delivered between November 1982 and February 1983.

The new buses were 668-702, with chassis built at Bristol, and not only were they 10.3m long 81-seaters, following the trial with the Preston Atlantean, but they had bodies built by ECW at Lowestoft, 388 miles from Edinburgh, rather than Alexander at Falkirk, just 33 miles from Edinburgh. The management at Alexander were naturally furious that they had not won this order, as their company had bodied every Edinburgh/Lothian double-decker since 1958.

Questions were asked at very high political levels about the wisdom of placing an order outside Scotland and putting local jobs at risk. But to no avail, and there would be several more batches of ECW Olympians to come. At the same time, Eastern Scottish, also based in Edinburgh, was also taking ECW-bodied Olympians – although these were shorter lowheight buses.

The first ECW Olympians were impressive beasts, with attractively styled bodies and an extra smaller-size side window on each deck to take account of the extra length. Internally, though, the seating and staircase arrangements were not ideal, with the stairs mounted immediately behind the driver, which meant that the stairs didn't line up with the exit door; this would be rectified on subsequent batches.

These buses were withdrawn in 2000.

No.673 reaches the top of the long climb up Kirk Brae at Liberton on the 7 service in June 1993.

Leyland and ECW delivered on their promise to supply the first batch of long Lothian Olympians quickly - all 35 were received within three months. Roger Hall photographed 690 in build at ECW's Lowestoft plant in January 1983. Note the short window bay to achieve the 10.3m length and the sloping Olympian radiator, normally hidden behind the ECW grille.

The 10.3m-long two-door ECW-bodied Olympians for Lothian contrasted with the recently-delivered 9.6m single-door lowheight ECW-bodied Olympians for Eastern Scottish. Two pose side by side at Holyrood during an Omnibus Society tour in March 1983. The Transign electronic destination on Lothian 702 was experimental; other buses in this first batch had conventional roller blinds.

No.670 in Princes Street in August 1983, when general traffic could use the street and The Mound junction was controlled by policemen. It carries the original style of Lothian livery, with gold LOTHIAN fleetname and Lothian crest, and displays a pro-bus advert on behalf of the Bus & Coach Council. Behind is a 1979 Eastern Scottish Leyland Fleetline, also with ECW bodywork.

MORE ECW OLYMPIANS

703-736   A-YFS   ONTL11/2R   ECW H51/32D

Lothian quickly fell into a pattern of ordering 30-odd new Olympians each year – batches of between 33 and 36 buses – which allowed for rolling replacement of the oldest buses and maintaining the fleet age profile.

The next order for ECW-bodied Olympians was for 34 and 703-736 arrived in October and November 1983. By placing seats behind the driver, the stairs were moved back and aligned with the centre door. The seating capacity was increased to 83.

The chassis of these and LRT's 1984-86 Olympians were assembled at Leyland's Workington plant in Cumbria, following the closure of the Bristol works.

These buses remained in service until 2000/01.

Edinburgh is a hilly city and here 734 of the second batch of ECW-bodied Olympians climbs Greenbank Crescent out of Comiston on a wintry day in January 1984.

A September 1996 rear view of freshly painted 729 showing the revised lower deck window layout following the decision to move the staircase back to face the centre door.

ECW-bodied Olympian 736 climbs The Mound on the 27 route in July 1995 followed by 313 from the 1988 Alexander-bodied batch.

No.711 breasts a hill on Restalrig Road South heading towards the city centre on the 19 service in May 2000.

MORE ECWs - AND THE FIRST 770

737-770   B-GSC   ONTL11/2R   ECW H51/32D

Exactly a year after the 1983 deliveries, 737-770 were placed in service. These were largely the same as 703-736.

Leyland required a demonstration vehicle to help it secure a large order in Thailand and a month after delivery to Lothian in December 1984 770 was delicensed and used by Leyland for demonstration purposes. It was exhibited at the UITP exhibition at Brussels in May 1985 and returned to Edinburgh the following month to enter service briefly with Lothian before sale to Leyland in July. It was refurbished to an export specification and sent to Thailand in 1987 but no orders followed. It ended up with Citybus in Hong Kong in 1990.

No.753 was transferred to the associated Mac Tours fleet in 2002 and was sold in 2004.

The rest of the 1984 batch were withdrawn in 2001/02.

With several Leyland Atlanteans and another Olympian in the background, 753 heads south down Craigmillar Park in June 1993.

Several of Lothian's Olympians were painted in overall advertising liveries. This one promoted bus travel on behalf of the Bus & Coach Council Scotland. With the Firth of Forth in the background 768 turns at its Newhaven terminus to start its long cross-city journey to Captains Road.

Only three years separate these Lothian buses – 1984 Olympian 755 and 1981 Leyland Atlantean/Alexander 638 – in North St Andrew Street, now part of route of the new Edinburgh tramway.

No.751 in April 1991 climbs Orchard Brae towards the city centre on its long trip to Penicuik, in Midlothian, pursued by one of the newly-delivered Leyland Lynxes.

Spot the Olympian. No.747 wears an allover advert for Hitachi, but gets rather lost against the Princes Street background.

Photographed by Bob McGillivray during its short stay in Edinburgh in 1985, Olympian 770 receives attention for overheating at Hyvot's Bank terminus – ironically it would soon be rebuilt by Leyland for much warmer climates in the hope of winning an order from Thailand.

The 1984 Olympian 770 worked with Lothian for only a short time before it was bought back by Leyland and fitted out as a demonstrator for business it hoped to win in Thailand. This proved unsuccessful and the bus was sold to Hong Kong Citybus in 1990. Note particularly the full-depth sliding windows, designed for a climate warmer than Edinburgh's. This is a Leyland Bus publicity photograph.

THE LAST ECWs

770-794	C-SFS	ONTL11/2R	ECW H51/32D

With the uncertainties of deregulation of local bus services on the horizon, the 1985 order was reduced to 25 buses, 770-794, delivered in December 1985 and January 1986. These included a second 770, replacing the 1984 version bought back by Leyland as a demonstrator. In total, ECW built 128 bodies on Leyland Olympian for Lothian between 1982 and 1986. No.777 is preserved.

These buses were withdrawn in 2001-04.

New and old – Olympian 780 and new Volvo B7TL/Plaxton President 295 in North St Andrew Street in May 2000. By this time, Lothian was using the fronts of its buses to promote its Day Ticket as well as a shorter-lived Off Peak Day Ticket. Buses no longer serve this street, which is now part of the new Edinburgh tramway.

Another contrast – Abbeyhill in September 2002, with Harlequin-liveried lowfloor Dennis Trident/Plaxton President 568, new in 2000, on the left alongside 1986 Olympian 793.

Body styles contrasted at Elm Row in May 2001 with ECW-bodied 774 and Alexander RH-bodied 349.

Now preserved by Lothian, 1985 ECW-bodied Olympian 777 is seen here in September 1996 in service in the Restalrig area on the 87 route to Penicuik in Midlothian. Following the deregulation of bus services in 1986, Lothian expanded successfully into East Lothian and Midlothian, as well as a brief foray into West Lothian.

BACK TO ALEXANDER

300-335   E-MSG   ONCL10/2RZ   ALEXANDER H51/30D

New bus deliveries in Britain plunged to low levels following deregulation in 1986 and after the delivery of the 1985/86 Olympians, Lothian took a purchasing holiday until April 1988, except for two single-deck coaches in 1986.

LRT's 1988 Olympians represented the biggest delivery of new buses in Scotland that year. And they were very different to their predecessors.

Leyland had closed its ECW plant at Lowestoft in 1987 so Lothian turned back to Alexander for its 1988 order – and for all of its future Olympians. These had RH type bodies to a similar outline to the 1982 Olympians, but with the small side windows on each deck to account for the extra length, and a new front panel under the deeper vee windscreen.

Underneath, 300-335 were different. They were ONCL10/2RZ models, signifying Cummins L10 engines in place of the Leyland TL11 unit, which had been phased out during the year, and ZF gearboxes. They were 81-seaters, as most of LRT's two-door Olympians would be over the next nine years. They were delivered in April/May 1988, on chassis built at the Leyland plant in Leyland, Lancashire; LRT's 1989-91 Olympian chassis would also be built at Leyland.

In 1999-2002, 14 (304-314, 333-335) of the 1988 Olympians were transferred to LRT's tour fleet, replacing Atlanteans and augmenting the company's successful open-top tour operation in Edinburgh. In 2000, 300-303 were transferred to Oxford to work Lothian's open-top operation there, returning to Edinburgh in 2002.

In 2002-2004 eight of the 1988 batch were transferred to driver training duties, with a 'TB' prefix added to their fleetnumbers to become TB315-322. No.TB315 was re-registered E422 RSC in 2007 to release E315 MSG for 1992 Olympian 875 in the tours fleet, which was being renumbered 315 to release the number 875 for a new Volvo B9TL.

In 2009 300-306/312-314/333-335 were renumbered 240-249/233-235 to release their original fleetnumbers for new Volvo B9TLs.

In 1988 Leyland Bus was bought by Volvo, which initially continued to produce the Olympian under the Leyland name. The service buses in this batch were withdrawn in 2005, the open-top examples between 2008 and 2011, and the driver training buses in 2009 and 2012. Trainer TB322 was retained by Lothian Buses and restored to its original condition as 322.

On the newly laid Greenway – for use only by buses and taxis at prescribed times of the day – 317 on the 14 service in July 1999 at the head of a trio of Olympians on Leith Walk. The 'LRT Lothian' via blind was a default setting in the absence of an appropriate set of intermediate points.

Proudly displaying its Leyland badge, 312 climbs from Tollcross past Bruntsfield Links bound for Oxgangs on the 16 route.

Fresh out of the box with side adverts yet to be applied, brand-new Alexander RH-bodied Olympian 305 proceeds from Waterloo Place into Princes Street in April 1988.

No.313 climbs The Mound from Princes Street in July 1995 with the Scottish National Gallery and the top of the Scott Monument to the right of the photograph.

In Princes Street in May 1988, 301 wears the short-lived LOTHIAN block capitals fleetname.

Eight 1988 Olympians were transferred to Lothian's driver training fleet. No.TB322, seen in Princes Street in September 2006, was retained by Lothian Buses and restored to its original condition.

BUSES
AND COACHES

336-345	G-CSG	ONCL10/2RZ	ALEXANDER H51/30D
346-365	F-WSC	ONCL10/2RZ	ALEXANDER H51/30D
366-371	F-WSC	ONCL10/2RZ	ALEXANDER CH47/31F

The next batch of Olympians included six single-door examples with coach seats for use on the Airport service and tours and hires, delivered in June 1989 as 366-371. The rest were 81-seat two-door buses delivered between May and August 1989, 336-365. The single-door buses were delivered in white/black coach livery, and in 1995 were repainted in blue/grey Airline livery then in 2000 in standard madder/white for normal bus duties. In 2005 they were painted bright red/white, mainly for use on the 15 route.

In 2004/05 336-338, 356-358 were transferred to Lothian's open-top tour fleet and in 2009 336-338 were renumbered 236-238 to make way for new Volvo B9TLs with these numbers. In 2003, single-door Olympian 371 was temporarily transferred to the associated Edinburgh Bus Tours fleet, returning to Lothian Buses in 2004.

The service buses were withdrawn in 2004-09 and the open-toppers in 2010/11.

Still sporting its prominent Leyland badge, 352 pulls away from the busy Elm Row stop on the 16 route to Hunter's Tryst.

The lighter red paint tried on some of the 1989 Olympians contrasts with the standard madder on ECW Olympian 777 and Leyland National 138 at Marine Garage in 2003.

Six of the 1989 Olympians were delivered as single-door buses with 78 coach seats, painted in the white/black coach livery. No.368 at Edinburgh Airport in May 1991 behind a Guide Friday Leyland Atlantean/East Lancs on the competing Airport service.

The six single-door Olympians later received this blue Airline livery. No.366 leaves the Airport passing a line of airport taxis waiting for custom. In recent years security concerns have moved taxis further from the Airport building. These buses would prove to be the longest survivors of Lothian's Leyland Olympians.

Lothian experimented with different paint colours in 2003/04 and some of the 1989 G-registered Olympians wore a range of lighter reds, like 342 in Hanover Street in May 2007.

ABOVE RIGHT: Newer buses for the Airport service replaced the 1989 coach Olympians in 1999, which were then painted in standard madder/white for bus duties, as seen on 367 in York Place. These spent much of their lives as buses on the lengthy 15 route to Penicuik.

RIGHT: In 2005 the six single-door Olympians received this brighter red/white livery for the long 15 service linking East Lothian and Midlothian via central Edinburgh. No.366 at Piershill in March 2009 carrying a 'tram board' showing extra via points, under the driver's windscreen.

No.360 turns out of Wakefield Avenue on the last stage of its journey to its King's Road terminus at Marine Garage in May 2007.

On 14 March 2009 Lothian Buses operated its last of 1,685 Leylands that had served the Edinburgh and Lothian fleets since 1919. The last Leylands, the single-door Olympians, carried these 'tram boards' marking the last day.

1990
DELIVERIES

800-835   G-GSX   ON2R56C13Z4 ALEXANDER H51/30D

In May-July 1990, 36 more two-door 81-seaters arrived, 800-835. Although the type designation had changed under Volvo control, the buses were still essentially the same as previous deliveries, and still badged as Leylands.

These buses were withdrawn in 2004-09.

Descending The Mound from Edinburgh's Old Town to the New Town in June 2006, 812 on a part route 23 heading only to Hanover Street.

The Tollcross landscape has changed greatly over the years, along with the buses. No.835 leaves Lauriston Place on the 23 in October 2004.

No.832 climbs Edinburgh's Royal Mile, with St Giles' Cathedral on the right. Buses are no longer able to pass this way as this part of the street has been largely pedestrianised.

The first of the 1990 batch of Olympians, 800, in Waterloo Place in June 1996, showing the higher-set rear emergency door. Note also the Leyland and Alexander badging; in more recent years Lothian chose to keep manufacturers' badges off its buses.

MORE STANDARD OLYMPIANS

836-871   J-TSC   ON2R56C13Z4 ALEXANDER H51/30D

Lothian received another 36 standard Olympians in August-November 1991, 836-871. Olympian chassis production returned from Leyland to Workington in 1991 and remained there until 1993.

The 1991 deliveries were withdrawn in 2007-09.

With a 'tram board' proclaiming the 1/6 Circle to be the Royal Mile Route, 840 is seen among the tenements of Easter Road in June 1999.

The 32 route was a lengthy (27-mile) Outer Circle route linking many of Edinburgh's suburbs on its 140-minute journey. No.869 crosses Junction Bridge in Leith in July 2003; the 'tram board' informs passengers that the 32 serves the newly-developed Fort Kinnaird shopping complex on the south-eastern fringes of the city.

With the Firth of Forth and the hills of Fife in the background, 854 turns from York Place into North St Andrew Street in June 2004, a manoeuvre that only trams have been able to make since 2014.

Climbing The Mound, 841 against the background of the Scottish National Gallery. The laurel wreath below the Lothian logo on the side proclaims that Lothian was voted the UK's Best Bus Company in 2003.

THE LAST LEYLANDS

872-887	K-CSF	ON2R56C13Z4	ALEXANDER	H51/30D
889-894	K-CSF	ON2R56C13Z4	ALEXANDER	H51/30D

Twenty-two standard Olympians followed between December 1992 and February 1993, 872-887/889-894 – the missing number 888 being unavailable as a registration from DVLA. No.875 was transferred to the tours fleet in 2005 and in 2007 was renumbered 315, taking the registration E315 MSG from a 1988 Olympian that was TB315 in the driver training fleet; this bus then gained the registration E422 RSC.

The 1992/93 Olympians were withdrawn in 2007-09, except for open-topper 315 (875), which was withdrawn in 2010.

No.880 on Regent Road in May 2008, preparing to take up a rush-hour journey, probably on one of the peak-hour limited stop services. To the left is Calton Hill and to the right is Holyrood Park.

No.873 poses outside the Walter Alexander coachworks in Falkirk in February 1993, marking the delivery of the 1,000th Alexander body for Lothian and its predecessor, Edinburgh Corporation. Alongside are two Dennis Darts with Alexander Dash bodies supplied at the same time. The K-registered batch would be Lothian's last Leyland Olympians; future deliveries would be badged as Volvos.

No.874 at the busy Elm Row crew changeover point, close to Lothian's Central Garage in Annandale Street, in May 2001 in the company of an older Olympian and a 2000-delivered Dennis/Plaxton SPD Dart on the high-frequency 22 service.

Olympian 890 descends The Mound towards Princes Street in 1992. The black-and-white bollards on the left of the bus were installed during tramway days to stop runaway trams plunging on to the railway line below.

THE FIRST VOLVOS

950-983   L-MSC   YN2RC16Z4   ALEXANDER H51/30D

Although the 34 Olympians delivered in February-April 1994, 950-983, were outwardly similar to previous deliveries, there were important differences. Visually, the main change was the introduction of rectangular rather than circular headlamps, but underneath, the chassis was a Volvo product, built at Irvine, Ayrshire, although they still retained Cummins L10 engines and ZF gearboxes. All subsequent Olympians would be built at Irvine. No.964 was fitted by Lothian with a more powerful Cummins M11 engine, and signs in the cab alerted drivers to the extra power.

The 1994 Olympians were withdrawn prematurely in 2006/07 as Lothian moved towards a commitment to field a fully-accessible lowfloor bus fleet by 2009.

Lothian's first Volvo Olympians were delivered in 1994 – externally the rectangular headlamps were the main clue. No.971 on the 44 route to Balerno at Leopold Place. Note the discreet Volvo and Alexander badging below the headlamps.

No.961 in Princes Street in July 2000 with an experimental and slightly squashed destination display, followed by a First Edinburgh Volvo Olympian/Alexander Royale.

Heading from Central Garage at Annandale Street to take up a journey on the 41 route, 972 navigates the roundabout at the junction of Leith Walk and Leopold Place in 2005.

Early evening in Princes Street in May 1999 as 960 picks up westbound passengers.

THE 1995 VOLVOS

201-221	M-VSX	YN2RC16Z4	ALEXANDER H51/30D
223-234	M-VSX	YN2RC16Z4	ALEXANDER H51/30D

Thirty-three more Volvo Olympians with Alexander RH bodies, 201-221/223-34 (DVLA was not issuing '222' registrations) were delivered in April-June 1995.

They were withdrawn in 2008/09, but 210 is preserved by Lothian Buses.

Descending The Mound past the Black Watch memorial, is 208 on the 46 Circle route. Although at one time Lothian had a few circular routes, problems with timekeeping meant that these were divided into more manageable services.

LEFT: Sporting Volvo and Alexander badges under its headlamps, 206 in Leith Walk in 1997 on its long journey to Penicuik.

BELOW LEFT: No.207 of the 1995 batch turns into Princes Street from South St Andrew Street in May 2006, a manoeuvre now restricted to trams. It carries the later white fleetnumbers and a brighter version of the madder/white livery with more white above the lower deck windows.

With the Royal Scottish Academy in the background, 201 passes the Scottish National Gallery on The Mound in April 2007 on its way to Blackford.

THE FIRST ROYALES

401-407	N-GSX	YN2RCV18Z4	ALEXANDER	H51/30D
408-420	P-KSX	YN2RCV18Z4	ALEXANDER	H51/30D
421-430	P-KSX	YN2RCV18Z4	ALEXANDER	H51/29D
431-433	P-KSX	YN2RCV18Z4	ALEXANDER	H49/27F

The next Volvo Olympians delivered to Lothian, between July and November 1996, were very different. They had Volvo TD102KF (later D10A) engines and Alexander's restyled body, named Royale. This was a less angular version of the RH type and the result was a very attractive bus. All future Lothian Olympian deliveries carried Royale bodies.

The first 30 were two-door buses, and the last 10 of these had modular rather than more traditional bus seats, reducing the lower deck capacity, and the overall seating capacity to 80. No.430 was rebuilt as a single door 84-seater in 2007; it was painted in a bright red/white livery in 2007, as were 431/432.

The last three of this batch were delivered as single-door 76-seaters for Airport, tour and hire work. Initially painted white/black, 431/432 later carried blue/grey/white Airlink colours and 433 became the bus for the X50 service to the former Royal Yacht Britannia, and then the bus for the Forth Bridges Cruise.

They were withdrawn in 2009, except for 433, which was withdrawn in 2011.

On its first day in service in July 1996, Volvo Olympian/Alexander Royale 402 at the Muirhouse terminus of the 14 route. Note the 'tram board' under the windscreen deputising for a 'via' blind. The Royale offered a more modern and rounded appearance than the RH type, on which it was based.

No.422 at Portobello Town Hall in May 2007, wearing the revised livery with more white relief. Behind is a Dennis Dart/Alexander working for Lothian's Mac Tours operation.

LEFT: Delivered in white/black livery for Airport service, 431 and 432 were repainted in blue/grey/white Airlink 100 livery in 1999, as seen on 432 turning from Princes Street on to Waverley Bridge in April 2001 to take up a journey on the X50 express service to Ocean Terminal in Leith where the former Royal Yacht Britannia is berthed.

Single-door 432, still with coach seating from its days on the Airport service and operating as a bus, turning from St Andrew Square into George Street in March 2009, diverted from Princes Street because of tramworks. It is wearing the red livery adopted for the 15 route.

Olympian Royale 420 was one of the buses used to test different paints and shades of red. At Junction Bridge, Leith in July 2003, the original madder can be seen where adverts have been removed – after painting – beside the destination display.

The upper deck of 402, when new in 1996, showing the practical, but rather clinical, seating and interior colour scheme, typical of Lothian buses at the time.

Olympian 416 descends The Mound in May 2008 on the 42 route against the backdrop of Princes Street, with the Scott Monument dominating the skyline.

LOTHIAN'S LAST OLYMPIANS

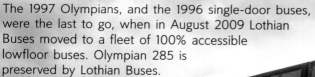

251-279	P-PSX	OLY-56	ALEXANDER H51/30D
281-285	P-PSX	OLY-56	ALEXANDER H51/30D

What would turn out to be the last of Lothian's 430 Olympians were 251-279/281-285 (DVLA didn't issue '280' registrations), delivered between May and July 1997. They were more Volvo-engined Royales, and by this stage the Olympian chassis designation had been simplified to OLY-56. Alexander had bodied 300 of Lothian's Leyland and Volvo Olympians between 1988 and 1997. The Olympian remained on the model lists, and the last complete bus for the UK market was delivered in August 2000. But by this time bus operators were moving to the new breed of lowfloor double-deckers and Lothian's next new double-deckers after the 1997 Olympians would be Dennis Tridents delivered in June 1999; after a few years standardising on Tridents, Lothian returned to Volvo in 2005 with its first orders what would become a substantial fleet of B7TL, B9TL, B5TL and B5LH chassis.

The 1997 Olympians, and the 1996 single-door buses, were the last to go, when in August 2009 Lothian Buses moved to a fleet of 100% accessible lowfloor buses. Olympian 285 is preserved by Lothian Buses.

No.255 on the 42 route in August 2007 commences its climb up Howe Street towards to city centre, on Edinburgh's notorious cobbles.

ABOVE LEFT: No.263 on the 15 in Queen Street in May 2009. Although it is billed as a 15, the tram board listing the intermediate points Bush and Milton Bridge refers to the 15A variant.

LEFT: No.278 sits outside Lothian's Shrubhill Works and head office in 1999, repainted and carrying adverts to launch the new bus priority Greenway routes around the city.

No.262 in an advertising livery for the local radio station passes work in progress on St Andrew Square for the new bus station and Harvey Nichols store.

On 29 August 2009, the last day of normal operation by Lothian's step entrance buses, 278 displays a 'tram board' marking the occasion.

At Abbeyhill in May 2009, Olympian 271, wearing its final livery style, passes a route-branded Trident/President on the 26 route.

GUIDE FRIDAY OLYMPIANS

40	C147 KBT	ONLXB/1R	OPTARE	CO47/29F	1985
41-43	A514/5/7 VKG	ONLXB/1R	EAST LANCS	O43/31F	1984
44-46	A156/8/9 FPG	ONTL11/1R	ROE	O43/29F	1984
47	A145 DPE	ONTL11/1R	ROE	O43/29F	1983
49	LBO 501X	ONLXB/1R	EAST LANCS	O43/31F	1981

Lothian Buses acquired more Olympians in 2002 when it took over the former Guide Friday operations in Edinburgh. Among the vehicles acquired were nine Olympians with bodies by East Lancs, Optare and Roe, and these were numbered 40-47/49 in the Lothian fleet. Five were ONLXB/1R models, signifying Gardner engines, which had been absent from the Edinburgh/Lothian fleet since the withdrawal of the last Guy Arab IVs in 1972.

No.40 was new to Yorkshire Rider in 1985. Nos.41-43/49 had originated with Cardiff City Transport in 1981 (49) and 1984 (41-43). No.49 was a very early Olympian – chassis ON44, which actually followed Lothian's 666/667, which were ON43 and ON42 respectively. Nos.44-47 were new to London Country in 1983 (47) and 1984 (44-46).

Several were repainted into Lothian's Edinburgh Tour and Majestic Tour liveries in 2002, and although some were sold fairly quickly, in 2003-05, some survived to 2008/09, though in the company's reserve fleet. All were sold on for further tourist service, and at least two ended up operating in the United States when they were well over 20 years old.

Edinburgh Castle looms over former Guide Friday Roe-bodied Olympian 47 as it climbs Johnston Terrace on an Edinburgh Tour duty in August 2003.

East Lancs bodied 42, sporting revised Edinburgh Tour livery, passes Roe bodied 45, in the older Guide Friday colours.

New to London Country in 1984, a former Guide Friday Roe-bodied Olympian in Lothian's Edinburgh Tour fleet as its 45, turns from Chambers Street on to George IV Bridge in August 2003.

Lothian introduced this blue/yellow livery for its Majestic Tour to the north of Edinburgh, taking visitors to the former Royal Yacht Britannia, moored at Ocean Terminal. No.49 is an ex-Cardiff Olympian/East Lancs which passed to Lothian with the Guide Friday fleet in 2002. It is seen on Waverley Bridge in August 2004.

OLYMPIANS IN THE TOUR FLEET

Lothian's predecessor, Edinburgh Corporation Transport, recognised the value of tourism right from the start of its bus operations, buying charabancs and small coaches in the 1920s. Conventional coaches were bought in the postwar years until competition from Guide Friday led to the conversion of a number of Leyland Atlanteans to open-top layout in 1989. The emphasis moved from local, UK and continental touring to developing the market for open-top tours and Lothian acquired its two competitors, Guide Friday and Mac Tours in 2002 and upgraded its tour fleet with converted Olympians, then lowfloor Dennis Tridents and more recently Volvo B5TLs.

The first Olympians to be converted to full open-top and semi open-top (with an enclosed section at the front of the upper deck) were in service on tours in 1999, with more conversions following in 2001-05.

Lothian was also involved in joint open-top operations in Cambridge, Oxford and York and four Olympians (300-303) were converted in 2000 for Oxford. These returned to the Edinburgh-based Lothian fleet in 2002.

Closed-top Olympians were also used on tours work. ECW-bodied 753 was transferred to the Mac Tours fleet in 2002; two RH types, 310/311, were used in closed-top form from 2001 and were converted to semi open-top in 2004; single-door Olympian 371 from the bus fleet was used on tour work in 2003/04 and then returned to the main service fleet; a later single-door Olympian, 433, joined the tours fleet in 2007 to operate the Britannia service and the Forth Bridges Cruise tour until it was replaced by a TransBus Trident for the 2012 season.

As Lothian introduced more tour brands the Olympians wore different liveries – City Sightseeing red, Edinburgh Tour green/cream, Majestic Tour blue/yellow and Mac Tours red/cream.

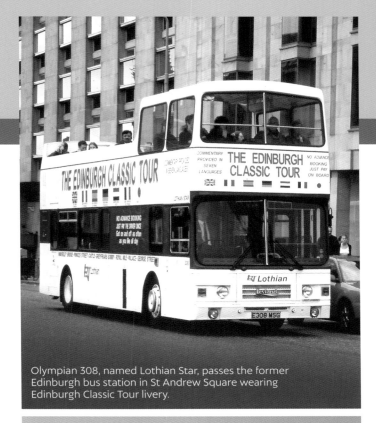

Olympian 308, named Lothian Star, passes the former Edinburgh bus station in St Andrew Square wearing Edinburgh Classic Tour livery.

No.308 was later repainted into City Sightseeing Edinburgh red livery. It is seen travelling along Princes Street.

To provide more covered accommodation for tour passengers, Lothian added an extra half-bay of roof to its partially open-top Olympians. No.314 descends the cobbles of the Lawnmarket in August 2003 in Edinburgh Tour colours.

The Majestic Tour took in the Royal Botanic Gardens and the former Royal Yacht Britannia, moored at Ocean Terminal in Leith. In April 2008 Olympian 358 crawls through the roadworks while Leith Walk was prepared for the new tramway – which has still to reach further north than York Place.

Open-top City Sightseeing Olympian 306 heads a line of open-toppers on Waverley Bridge, including Olympians in Majestic Tour and Edinburgh Tour liveries and a long Routemaster in Mac Tours colours.

ECW-bodied Olympian 753 was transferred to the Mac Tours fleet in 2002 to provide a free service to the Edinburgh Crystal factory in Penicuik. It is seen on Waverley Bridge.

No.310 ran briefly as a closed top City Sightseeing vehicle, but was soon converted to semi-open-top layout. It is in Princes Street in March 2004. Alongside is a Mercedes-Benz Vito minibus on Stagecoach's pioneering demand-responsive Yellow Taxibus service between Edinburgh and Dunfermline.

Lothian offered a bus and boat tour, the Forth Bridges Cruise, giving visitors the opportunity to view the bridges during a short cruise on the Forth. Olympian 433 at Waverley Bridge in April 2007.

SOLD FOR FURTHER SERVICE

For a number of years Lothian Region Transport had a policy of scrapping all of its surplus buses, so relatively few of its Leyland Atlanteans ended up with new owners. Management changes brought fresh thinking and Lothian Buses realised that its well-maintained buses were a valuable asset that would find ready customers around the UK – and indeed beyond.

When withdrawal of the ECW-bodied Olympians started in 2000, after 17 years service, they were snapped up by operators of all sizes, and this situation continued as the Lothian Olympian fleet shrank.

As Lothian bought longer and therefore higher-capacity Olympians than most operators, its 81-seaters were popular for school bus work, particularly if the centre door was removed and the lower deck seating capacity increased accordingly.

Lothian Olympians even found their way overseas, for example to Budapest, where they operated open-top tours, and to Australia, where four Royales provided visitors the chance to enjoy the Blue Mountains.

Two former Lothian ECW Olympians from the fleet of Marbill, Beith return to Edinburgh's George IV Bridge in August 2003 on private hire duties connected with the Edinburgh Military Tattoo. Marbill bought 39 former Lothian Olympians.

Blackburn Transport invested in 23 Lothian ECW-bodied Olympians in 2000-02 and 11 are lined up in the Blackburn depot in September 2007, by which time the Blackburn municipal operation had been acquired by Blazefield.

Two former Lothian Volvo Olympians were used by Stagecoach on the shuttle service from the centre of Edinburgh to the experimental ForthFast hovercraft service linking Portobello and Kirkcaldy in July 2007. The buses were provided by Horsburgh, Pumpherston and former Lothian 973 is on Waverley Bridge.

BELOW LEFT: The former Lothian 683 in service in Sheffield in June 2001 with the local independent, Powell's Bus Co of Rotherham.

BELOW CENTRE: Preston Bus bought 10 Lothian Olympians, which passed to Stagecoach following its acquisition of the company in 2009; ex-Lothian 324 is seen in Preston in February 2010. Stagecoach was forced to divest the Preston business to Rotala in 2011 following competition concerns.

BELOW RIGHT: TrentBarton bought 17 ex-Lothian Olympians for its Notts+Derby operation; former Lothian 865 at Derby bus station in September 2011.

Former Lothian 303 in service with Big Bus in Budapest in August 2013. The UK centre door has been removed and repositioned ahead of the rear axle on the right-hand side of the bus. Photo by Keith McGillivray.

The West Lothian independent E & M Horsburgh bought 28 of Lothian's withdrawn Olympians, taking both ECW and Alexander examples; ex-Lothian 786 is seen on Princes Street in August 2005 working Lothian's 100 Airport service during a drivers' strike.

Four ex-Lothian Royale Olympians were exported to Australia for use on Blue Mountains Explorer Bus tours around Katoomba, New South Wales. They retained their Lothian fleetnumbers, as in this 2013 view of the former Lothian 273 – the others are 251, 264 and 270. Photo by Ross Scoular.

Local preservationist, Calum Melrose, has produced these images showing how the Lothian Olympian progressed from the two prototypes, top left, to the final Royales, by way of the ECW-bodied examples and the Alexander RH type deliveries.

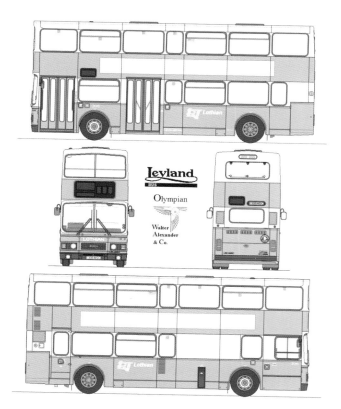

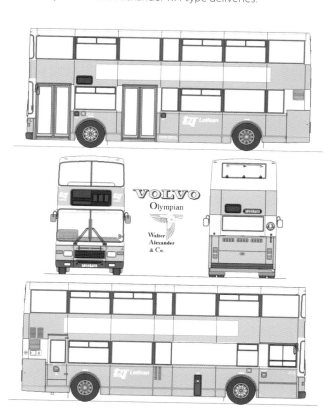

OLYMPIANS IN PRESERVATION

Fortunately, at least five Lothian Olympians are preserved by Lothian Buses – prototype 667, ECW 777, Leyland/Alexander RH type 322, Volvo/Alexander RH type 210 and Volvo/Alexander Royale 285. Lothian Buses has used its preserved Olympians on special services to the Royal Highland Show and the annual Gardening Scotland exhibition, both at Ingliston. Nos.285 and 322 were used as peak-hour extras on the busy 25 route linking Haymarket and Riccarton Campus until September 2016 and in September 2017 short-workings on the 26 route between Eastfield and Haymarket to coincide with the annual Open Day at Lothian's Central Garage were operated by 285, 322, 667 and 777.

No.322 of 1988, a Leyland Olympian/Alexander RH type, has been retained by Lothian Buses and restored to its original condition – it had latterly been a driver training bus. It is seen in September 2017 in St Andrew Square operating an Open Day short working between Eastfield and Haymarket.

Preserved 1985 ECW-bodied Leyland Olympian 777 leaves Eastfield terminus for Haymarket in September 2017 on a special 26 working tied in with the Open Day at Lothian's Central Garage. A preserved Leyland National sits in the turning circle.

One of the two prototype Leyland Olympians, 667 with Alexander body, has been preserved by Lothian Buses. It is seen here at the Scottish Vintage Bus Museum at Lathalmond, Fife.

Keith McGillivray photographed three of Lothian's preserved buses at Marine Garage the night before the start of the 2017 Royal Highland Show when they were used on the special service linking the city centre and the showground at Ingliston. Olympians 322 and 285 flank 2000-delivered Dennis Trident/Plaxton President 572.